I0540087

Publishing for the first time
in The Journal

Contents

3

6

8

15

18

21

22

32

Don Loop

Fall Of The Year

Well, ol' sol' is hauling south again,
Or, the earth is wobbling orth…
Whatever! Fall we understand.
Chrysanthemums we set forth

And welcome cooler, dryer air
That lets us drink out on the porch
Without the sick mosquito scare
Or the citronella torch.

'When the frost is on the punkin,'
O' course, up north snide Boreas
Is preparing snow for our dunkin.'
Global warming evaporates

More water for the cold jet stream
To turn into snow, they say. We'll see.
Meanwhile we'll bank that frosty scene
And watch the flowers retrocede.

Dead leaves fall down and blow about
And birds that migrate go south.
We think of cider and apple pie.
Love birds are breathin' sigh on sigh!

It's fall again.

Joyce Stedelbauer

Chambered Nautilus

My heart is a Chambered Nautilus curled in spiraled beauty, storm-tossed in
tempestuous seas, suddenly
stranded on an unfamiliar reef near a smack of jellyfish.
A pod of seals suns nearby while overhead
a flight of kestrels keens over this uncharted ocean.

My love and I reveled in star-strung nights;
sun-soaked days from here to Lilongwe and back again.
We began growing together filling each chamber with adventurous purpose,
adding another and another,
lifting and lowering with the rhythm of the tides.

The thin thread of life, a long filament wound around family and friends
sharing strength and sorrows,
polishing our private shell to its luminous luster as if the mysterious moon
laid down a new mantle
of nacre with each rising and setting.

Now I must sail alone without my captain but sail I must---
into thrusting winds---trusting that my circled shell is strong enough not
to shatter against
rebellious rocks.

Sharon Canfield Dorsey

The Secret Life Of Sleeping Beauty

(A Narrative Poem)

She lay very still in her glass casket, eyes closed, waiting.
The clip-clop of horses' hooves drew nearer, then stopped.
Dry leaves crunched under Prince Charming's feet.
A fragrant breeze stirred Sleeping Beauty's blonde curls

as the prince carefully lifted the flower-covered lid.
Beauty held her breath, willing her body to be still.
Charming was overcome by her delicate beauty.
He bent down and gently touched her lips with his.

Nothing happened. Beauty did not awaken.
Once more, he kissed her. Nothing.
Presuming her to be dead, an anguished Charming
rode away into the depths of the thick forest.

When all sounds had faded into the distance,
Beauty climbed from her golden casket and
ran in the opposite direction, stopping only long enough
to trade the frilly gown for a pair of pants and linen shirt.

Tucking her long hair under a cap, she could easily
pass for a young boy, out for a walk in the countryside.
She retrieved her notebook from its hiding place and
sat down to finish her story…

"Once upon a time, there was a young woman who
didn't want to marry Prince Charming or become a princess.
Instead, she wanted to write books about magic spells,
wicked witches and damsels who didn't need rescuing."

Sharon Canfield Dorsey

Tightrope

Life is like walking a tightrope.

We embark on the journey with confident enthusiasm.
We reach the middle just trying not to fall off.

We approach the end with hard-won wisdom that the
tightrope walkers behind us don't want to hear.

Rescue

I watch them creep across the slippery ledge,
staying close, one behind the other, soldiers on patrol.
The rescuer in front stops to check on a fallen comrade,
leans over him for a long moment, then moves on.

Three more times he pauses, leans over,
then moves past the still bodies, his guard following,
each of them careful not to get too close
to the edge of the precipice.

The fifth time they pause, there is movement.
Quickly, the guard comes forward.
The rescuers place themselves on either side
of the wounded and carry him to the edge of the ledge.

A chain of helpers passes him down, one by one,
'til he is safely on the ground.
As I watch them carry him into the tall grass,
I find myself wishing humans were as compassionate as ants.

Jim Gordon

Baptism

He bathed

in

the baptism

of

the wounds…

both his and theirs

and

from

the ashes

there came

a Passion

for

Life.

love divine

The quickening of your body

awakes my vital touch

that reunites that longing

I've come to love so much.

To smell

to breathe

to fill

with Energy

from

a greater well.

The honor is mine

The beauty of love divine.

DON LOOP grew up in Blacksburg, Virginia. He joined the US Navy and served aboard submarines. Following service in the navy he attended Lynchburg College and St. Johns in Annapolis, MD. Don has had a split commercial career, which included years in life insurance sales and management, and building construction specializing in residential, commercial renovation and historical restoration as well as home building.

Arriving in Urbanna, VA on a sailboat, he makes his home there, and is blessed with a son, daughter and three grandsons.

JOYCE CARR STEDELBAUER is an author and poet who lives in Williamsburg, Virginia. She is the author of four popular inspirational books on biblical people: *Have You Met Eve?, Have You Seen the Star?, Who Rolled the Stone?*, and *Where are you Adam?*

She has written two children's books: *Awesome Alphabet Animal's Party* and *Angels Birthday Celebration.*

SHARON CANFIELD DORSEY is the author of three children's books, a memoir, and a book of poetry. She has received awards from the CNU Writer's Conference, Poetry Society of Virginia, Gulf Coast Writer's Association and Chesapeake Bay Writers. Her poems are also included in an anthology by the James City Poets, titled, *Captured Moments*. She is a Senior Sales Director of thirty-eight years with Mary Kay Cosmetics.

Visit her website: www.SharonCanfieldDorsey.com.

J. BLACKWELL GORDON Captain Jim resides in a Mill Creek cottage on Virginia's Chesapeake Bay enjoying boating, sailing and kayaking. A love of the sea enriches his unique approach. He is the author of *Songbook From My Soul, Notes of the Sea, Gutsy Tales of the Rails, Living Out Loud*, and *Who Let the Crabs Out, Navigating the Waters of Life*. For more information, go to www.SuccessfulLifeSailing.com.

"Within each person is the seed of greatness."

Of Money and Luck

Alec Ream

Courtesy: Wikipedia

This railroad had its origins as the Lake Tahoe Railroad, an 8.75-mile, narrow-gauge line that ran from the lumber mills at Glenbrook to the head of the flume at Spooner Summit to the northeast. Built by Darius O. Mills and Henry M. Yerington of the Virginia and Truckee Railroad and banker Duane L. Bliss, the little line began operations Aug. 23, 1875, making an average of six lumber runs a day until the end of the cutting season in November 1898. The mines of the Comstock Lode -- the primary market for Lake Tahoe Basin timber -- were nearly all closed down by the time and the lands had been stripped of trees.

Recreational activities at the lake were heavily advertised in Reno and San Francisco and as many as four excursions a day were conducted. The Glenbrook and other engines ran out on the Tahoe Tavern pierwhere passengers could debark and board a waiting ship for a cruise around the lake.

It was January 1905, and Lise LaBonté found herself in an enviable situation. She wanted for nothing and her status was due, in part, to a winning streak. She was the belle of the Tahoe gambling set and was seriously considering buying the Lake Tahoe Railway. After all, it carried her from San Francisco to Tahoe in style, two weekends a month – although lately, it was four. At the age of twenty-eight, she had already attended and vamoosed from Miss Porter's, a back east finishing school. Despite her departure, she was presented at the San Francisco Cotillion as a debutante. Still single at twenty-eight, she was considered an old maid by social yardsticks… and the clock was ticking if she were to produce an heir to the family fortune.

On Saturday evenings she attended her mother's Congregation Emanu-El- a Jewish Temple that was a rarity in San Francisco, and Sunday she would arrive at Trinity Episcopal Church in Pacific Heights on her father's arm. Her age was becoming an issue. Therefore, the pressure was on to find a nice Jewish boy, one from a proper family with the appropriate credentials. It was a tiring schedule, but she rigidly adhered to it in order to please her parents.

Tahoe became her only respite, the Lake Tahoe Railway her transport, and gambling her salvation. Lise had even created an education fund for the train's hostesses, the *Zephyrettes*. She had cash, appreciated the gratitude of those she aided, and was ever in search of adventure as she was stunned by her boredom. So stunned that she often stared into the fog on the train window from her own breath, leaning into the glass to baptize herself with the cold, and imagined a shivering poverty she'd never known.

When not travelling to Tahoe, she would often

spend one night a week at the St. Francis Hotel in San Francisco for one reason only: *it was not home*. Her place on Telegraph Hill was lovely, the *hors d'oeuvre* and salon conversation legendary, and Lise may have been there physically, but her mind was always in Tahoe. Nobody understood, and this she tenderly, frequently regretted. Gambling was exciting, though. Gambling brought relief from the stupefied boredom. It was at the St. Francis that she met Kyle Crocker, a young hotelier with everything *but* money. A nice Jewish boy, he came from a notable family. His cousins owned the Southern Pacific Railroad and had built the St. Francis where he lived in a fine room on the third floor. The room was provided to him in exchange for his diligent labor. He was visible but indistinguishable from the staff at the hotel as he wore a uniform and worked the front desk. He wanted for nothing; he knew his lot in life and was content.

Except for one thing: Kyle wanted Lise. Week in and week out, from behind a gold-flecked marble counter, he checked her in and checked her out. No scandal; Kyle was devout and conscientious – why, his cousins (who trusted no one) trusted him.

Saturdays saw him at Congregation Emanu-El. He kept a wandering eye on Lise, and following worship and after the traditional coffee and pastry, he had a habit. He'd carry the trash out. Sort of a rite of consternation - *because everyone thinks highly of me, except me*. His poor dad had helped him form his low self-esteem. Most nights in his early years were marked by homelessness due to his father's addictions, and they had spent their lives out on the streets.

Despite his belief that Lise did not notice him, she was intrigued by his black hair and sturdy build. She did know all about him; his cousins came to socials at her home. She wanted to know him; her dark green eyes merged with his blue eyes like a lush continent to a white cap sea. It was just that her parents were old fashioned people; kind, lovely folks who were concerned about her welfare. Whenever she'd mention someone ambitious, her mother and father had a certified meltdown. Words like *insubstantial* and *climber* and *gold-digger* flew from their lips like cherry blossoms in a spring breeze. Part of her opposed them; part of her agreed. Lise was

conflicted, complex, and given to genius. She was an expert at counting cards up at the Tahoe poker tables, and that's one way she won.

Rebellion to her folks explained her departure from Miss Porter's prior to graduation, and rebellion accounted for her excursions to the Tahoe gambling parlors and her risking the family fortune. So far, though, she'd doubled her share of the San Joachin plantation money.

Her agreement with them was that she would find a suitable husband, one that was not a gold digger. That promise kept them at bay, and they said little of her Tahoe excursions. So, she did not act on her interest in Kyle as her fear that Kyle was a trick-or-treater, complete with a uniform costume, would violate their trust. After all, they could cut her off without a cent if they felt it would dissuade an unscrupulous suitor.

So, despite her interest, his blue eyes, and the fact the years were gaining on her, she decided it was not worth the gamble.

Too bad, she thought. *It would be nice to sit beside someone with a reflective disposition who did not feel the need to babble on about nonsense*, she reflected as she stared at snowy Auburn through a misty train window.

***

The nagging thought - *If I forget living on the streets, I may end up back there* – replayed itself in Kyle's head at every opportunity. He sought relief from that fear in toiling at his cousin's hotel. He worked, was housed, fed, even clothed at the St. Francis Hotel on Union Square. On one hand, luxury surrounded him...this was comforting. On the other hand, the stout presence of physical work bothered him as there was always some labor to do at the St. Francis. Kyle could go from clerk to repairman at the bat of the hotel manager's eye. That work, often out in the cold, damp San Francisco air increased his anxiety. It was the memory of those cold streets from his childhood that kept him in his place.

Which makes the curious thing that took place on this particular day the more striking. Done with clerking the desk, done with a repair or two, Kyle went for his nightly walk down Post, Grant and Sutter. As usual, 15 minutes in, he stopped on the sidewalk to admire the neoclassic lines of The White House department store. *I live and work here now, near where we begged: right here.* Almost a minute after, still walking, he passed an alley on Grant to see a scruff of a man shambling into the shadow. Kyle heard his frame fall to the gravel, then heavy breath. He quickened his step, in concert with his heartbeat. *Get gone fast. One step, down the curb, six fast steps across, ahead to the sidewalk, keep walking, then stop.* Was it divine intervention that stopped Kyle that evening? Or was it the longing to be rid of his fear from his childhood days, begging on the streets?. *What if I don't have to...fret myself, anymore... with fear? What if the bad is...already over, done with?*

Kyle walked into the dark. He knelt to one knee, picked up the darker form by an arm, and looped in around his shoulder. He rose up, dragging the semiconscious figure to its feet. "No hospital," the fellow pled; the murmur was almost indecipherable. "No hospital," the man repeated, this time in Kyle's left ear.

"Okay, friend. But you need to walk."

So, off they went surrounded by the slight smell of alcohol and the heavy smell of blood. *Just a friend of mine Officer,* Kyle's subconscious rehearsed, in case he needed. He didn't though, nor did he worry, at least not about that. He was more concerned about how to get into the hotel and bandage his patient without taxing his cousins' trust to scandalize himself - not just out of a job - but out of a decent life. Practically though, so far, it was working; at least the wayfarer could now move his feet.

Sutter St...Grant Ave...Post...and Powell. Kyle had acquired a military cadence during the longest 20 minutes he had ever known. *How the hell am I going to get him into my room without being seen?* Kyle changed his rhythm to *late ...shoulder... hit... bullet... bloody...late.* On they marched, Kyle dragging and coaxing the man to his feet.

Finally, they had arrived at the St. Francis. Kyle lived on the 3rd floor, and decided to risk the servant's elevator accessed through the back of the building. His rescued comrade probably couldn't manage the stairs, and Kyle (fit as he was) was running out of steam. It was midnight; the fellow was talking, his name was John, and he had a .38 caliber in the right deltoid. Kyle was prepared for events such as these;

many times, he pulled bullets from members of the staff. He had some whisky for special occasions, a pocket knife, tweezers, a pewter lighter, and some clean t-shirts.

He went to work.

***

Roulette had paid off; Lise had studied the wheel before betting. She considered it a refreshing break from the poker and black jack tables. At the card tables she was surrounded by moneyed-up *both or and* choices. The whole purpose was to fake your hand to deceive your opponents. Decisions for her were never sharp, they were never *either-or*. Never cut and dried. Roulette was sharp. It offered either black or red, odd or even, and high or low. After several hours and substantial winnings, she decided to retire to her cottage.

Her grandfather had introduced her to roulette with his friend, George Bernard Shaw. Grandfather had quoted Shaw after the flush of his first big roulette win, "The roulette table pays nobody except him that keeps it. Nevertheless, a passion for gaming is common, though a passion for keeping roulette tables is unknown."

The spruce wood fire in her Tahoe cottage burned bright and smelled fresh. She turned off the gas, robed up, and made a blanket fortress on the couch. It wasn't snowing as hard now, and she heard the sound of the room service cart being carefully wheeled down the cloister on a stone and slate covered walk. She checked her watch. It had been a mere 15 minutes since she had called for Manhattan Shrimp Chowder, French bread and room-temperature Merlot.

***

Kyle was also gambling in a high-stakes game. After all, he had worked hard to get off the streets. John was the reminder of what awaited if he failed.

He knew what his choice involved: either not help John and turn him out on this cold night to a certain death, or help him heal by removing the bullet and provide his services to an outcast from his old world. He studied John, slumped at his table drinking cold water mixed with a bit of coffee. Kyle sipped his whisky. Finally, he lit a candle to the blade of the knife to sterilize it.

"I know beggars can't be choosers," John began. "But do you know what you're doing? And you must be rich, so why pull beggars from the streets?"

"My cousins own the place, and our family's high caliber," Kyle replied grimly. "I work for my lodging and meals and spending money. I was once you, well as a child anyway."

John started to smile, then winced.

"So, this is me helping you...by hurting you," Kyle ventured. Delt got hit from behind. That's good - more chance for a muscle hit, less for bone."

"How will you know?" John said, putting his head to his hand.

Kyle placed the bottle before him, with a careful sound of glass on mahogany.

"You'll need some. Don't drink yourself onto the floor," he muttered.

John started to sass back, loud. "Sorry, you can't yell; St. Francis folks. Bite on this," Kyle said as he shoved a town rang into John's mouth. "Grew up on the streets, dad died there. I'm not going back. Looks like a .45 cal bullet."

John sat back a bit. "Good thing it's not a Colt M1900. Used them in the Philippines, not worth a damn, but made a bigger hole. Army went back to .45 cal."

"Do you know the guy?" Kyle asked as he cut the bullet hole longer. "Never mind. I'm only doing this once; no double jeopardy. One cut."

John leaned forward to drink again before the field surgery. "Right."

Kyle pried open the wound to see the bullet. He reached for the tweezers and his thumb and forefinger slipped. The wound started to close. John was good about it.

Kyle took another shirt, dried the wound, took some salt, and said he was sorry once more. John froze from searing pain. "Drink more and give it to me," Kyle directed. John did and whisky went on the salted wound. Kyle thought of a hot metal hiss of steam and felt like he could hear it.

One more clean shirt and the wound was dry for a sliver of time. He pried it open to view the lead. The tweezers were in reach, the skin dry. Bullet came plumb out.

"Hold still pal." Some bourbon to wash the wound, and the thread got soaked in the last of it. Kyle held the needle over the flame and plunged it into the swollen flesh, carefully stitching the wound closed.

***

Lise touched the fringe of the tartan blanket that covered the quilt on her lap, carefully tucking her legs beneath the two layers. She leaned against the couch's embroidered arm and smelled the burning spruce. Beyond the cold glass of the window was the snow. She pondered the cold and took a drink from the glass. The chowder was done; she'd saved her bread for dessert. She was smart that way, in the application of the liberal arts. Bread becomes sugar; bread's a good dessert.

The fire shone through the Merlot, bright and dark and dry. She felt a twinge as she looked out the window once more; in the cloister of cottages there was a winter cardinal, bright red. Wondering about one hardworking Kyle Crocker, she broke some bread, sipped some wine and wondered what poet should be read at the discussion salon of the upcoming Cotillion *Debutante*, at the St. Francis.

***

John had passed out, partly from the pain, and surely because of the whiskey. He jerked awake, and looked around. His eyes strayed to Kyle. "I need to get out of here. The thing is - you can't get fired because of me," John mumbled.

"That won't happen," Kyle asserted, "and I'll tell you why. My cousins offered me either daily maid service or free room service on Shabbat. I chose the latter. Nobody comes here. Long as you don't order food when I'm at Emanu-El you're good. You can stay here for a week or two. Keep quiet and ship out. No problem."

"I'm not used to staying in another place," John replied.

Kyle grew quiet. "I know how that is," he finished quickly.

"I got a lawyer," John volleyed. "He's making the preparations."

"Preparations?" Kyle repeated. A few moments passed.

"My son and his stepmother," John exasperated.

"My first wife came from money. From the gold mine. And I inherited it all when she died. I got money. My own son wants me dead and knows I won't shoot back at him. She doesn't care. He's just like her."

Kyle didn't want to reply, so he parroted John. "You don't have a place to live, are on the streets… and he shot you?" Kyle took the scissors out of the drawer along with fresh gauze.

"He shot me at the lawyer's. No, I have a home on the Nob. He shot him, after me. He's in a coma, at Park Hospital. I ran…well, crawled, to the alley where you found me. Ran or he would have finished me off."

Nob Hill. Near his cousin's house where the railroad barons known as the big four — Charles Crocker, Leland Stanford, Mark Hopkins and Collis Huntington — in the 1870s had built their mansions. Close on their heels came the bonanza kings of the Comstock Lode, James Flood and James G. Flair.

Their architectural excesses were such that the lowlanders came in droves to stare. "The hill of palaces" was how Robert Louis Stevenson described the scene in 1882.

"So, you have a house on Nob Hill?" Kyle queried.

"Yes, family home. My grandfather made his fortune in the 1848 gold strike. My grandmother insisted he build up there. She believed the scrub-covered hill offered an escape from the rowdiness of San Francisco. That 376 feet above the waterfront he thought would protect her. My father inherited the house, and I did upon his death in 1892. Now, my son is in line to inherit. His stepmother is trying to speed up the process."

The phone rang, but Kyle was looking for alcohol in the cabinet and didn't answer it. "So, John. Stay here for the next few days. You are safe here, and we're about the same size. I'll fetch some clothes for you, you can bathe and relax. We'll get rid of these bloody things…" Kyle's voice trailed off as he stuffed John's filthy clothing into a pillowcase. "I'll be gone for the afternoon tomorrow hiking on Half Dome. I only work a half day. Then I'll be back tomorrow night for the Cotillion: my cousins' little *soirée*. Brother you got nothing to worry about."

"Yeah I was invited to that. This Saturday," John added.

***

"Good morning Ma'am. What may we help you with?" Kyle asked, noticing the sun-kissed browns on the black straight hair falling behind her shoulders. Her eyes were green, and her hair set them a-shimmer.

"Good morning, and thank you," Lise replied. "I'd like my usual room. And, if you'd pass a note to Mrs. Crocker?" Kyle took a pen and a pad of paper in his hand. "Emily Dickinson will be read at the afternoon discussion before the Cotillion."

"And the food," Lise noted. Kyle turned a page on his pad of hotel stationery. "Palm hearts," she began, "…thin squared Havarti…square celery slices with chicken salad," she continued, "…butter baked water crackers, brie and raspberry. Any dry champagne; Mrs. Crocker's favorite will be fine."

***

John's son, Davidson, with stepmother in tow, was staying on the Piedmont side of Oakland. They had gone back to the house on Nob Hill cleaning out what they could carry back to the hotel. His stepmother then visited Park Emergency to ensure John's lawyer was still in a coma. No one knew that she had pulled the trigger to shoot the barrister as Davidson was shooting his father. *Should have shot John myself. That buffoon Davidson only grazed his shoulder.*

John, still stupefied and ashamed of being found shot and drunk in an alley, was quiet. Afraid for his life, he'd stay quiet.

Davidson lined the cocaine on the cherry butler's tray and snorted deep, sharp and quick. *Lawyer = trouble* unless…

He ruminated over his plan to kill his father. His stepmother took every opportunity to remind him he had failed. From the shadows on Grant Street, he'd seen Kyle pick his father up to start walking and struggling. That thought made him sick. He took another snort of coke. Tailing the two at a distance, he'd seen them enter the service door of the hotel. Then standing in the alley, he stared at the panorama of the St. Francis, watching the window lights and estimating the service elevator. No new lights came on, then one did, third floor, fifth room, right of center. He traced a corner of the cotillion invitation across his index finger and found some dirt under the nail. He and his new lady wouldn't go, but his buddy could - to create a nice diversion.

All that cornice work on the St. Francis, all that corner stone detail. Three floors would be no piece of cake, but well worth a godless goldmine. Davidson would be the god, and that was better than cocaine.

***

Kyle rolled his canvas drop cloth along the floor for a third time. He pressed a knee to the roll with each turn to ensure its resourcefulness in his backpack. He needed room for some Brunswick stew in a sealed crock from the hotel kitchen, his bourbon, then the boiled shrimp he'd cold packed for his lunch.

"Sure, you don't want to head downstairs to the hootenanny?" Kyle asked.

"Back in the day," John replied thoughtfully.

***

Davidson's partner in cocaine walked into the salon. He'd just set a timed distraction in the water closet adjacent. Mme. LaBonté stood to read Dickinson before a room of 30 women in the first three rows. White dresses with pastel satin sashes. The men were seated in the last rows to bring *hors d'oeuvres* and wine during the discussion.

Because I could not stop for Death
He kindly stopped for me;
The carriage held but just ourselves
And Immortality

The stonework relief on the walls of the St. Francis was such that Davidson didn't really need to use a climbing claw, but it exalted himself to do so all the same.

We slowly drove, he knew no haste
And I had put away,
My labor and my leisure too,
For His Civility

Davidson felt a surge of overexertion that seamlessly morphed into self-congratulation.

We passed the School, where childred played,
Their lessons scarcely done;
We passed the fields of gazing grain,
We passed the setting sun.

Second floor - hustling - if you exhale thoroughly, inhaling takes care of itself.

We paused before a house that seemed
A Swelling of the Ground;
The Roof was scarcely visible,
The cornice but a mound.

Third floor, fifth window. The ball of a furious right foot loosed a crude triangle of glass to slice the guy on the couch. He reflexed straight to his wound. This facilitated his vulnerability to the second. And the knife went deep - more than enough blood.

Since then 'tis centuries; but each
Feels shorter than the day
I first surmised the horses' heads
Were toward eternity.[1]

***

Fifteen minutes earlier, Kyle was on the curb, holding a backpack. December bay winds were temperate..A cousin's Packard arrived; the driver put it in Park.

"Here you are Mr. Crocker," the driver said brightly. Kyle heard the noise of busy traffic; it made him feel privileged knowing the street noise was a temporary inconvenience. In his youth the same street sounds had tortured him.

"Mr. Crocker!" a woman spoke heavily from the revolving door. "It's the ballroom bathroom!"

Kyle looked at the Packard, then toward her. "God," he exhaled, wrenching a swear to a prayer.

He handed the backpack to the driver and sauntered into the St. Francis.

The smoke and stench weren't limited to the washroom. Inside Kyle was nauseous and overcome. His stomach splattered gold bile to the black and white octagonal tiled floor. Staggering to a stall with a device fastened to the porcelain edge, he stomped a smoke bomb into the soiled water, soaking his shoe,

---

1 The version of Emily Dickson's poem used in this story is her original published posthumously in *Poems: Series 1*, 1890. There are other versions in common use today, including the Close transcription. The modern transcription was published until 1999. Therefore, we are using the format in the *Poems*: Series publication as it was the version available during the time period in this piece.
Source: Wikipedia

then flushed.

The poetry salon was bereft of dignity and much beside itself. A few fathers were insisting, loudly, on refunds.

This isn't the half of it, Kyle thought, considering the last few days. *This **is not** the half of it*, he thought again, sprinting the stairs up to the elevators. A second floor elevator was open. Inside, he stomped his soaking foot in the elevator to subdue some nervous piss. The elevator sconces blinked at the reverberation, then the door opened. Running to his room, he fumbled with the keys till he screamed in agony, dropping them. He kicked in the door to see John bleeding. Profusely. Kyle knelt and pressed his hand to the cavity.

My Lord and God! Kyle agonized. John's head turned.

"Lawyer woke," John announced. "Mine's yours. I was writing it out in this will. Right here. House too. Don't know how…" his voice trailed off.

John was dead. Davidson lay next to him. Kyle lost his dignity and wept till he hollered out loud.

Blood, water and salt.

The first-floor fecal smell conceded its offensiveness to the shrill sound of sirens. Someone was dead at the St. Francis, in the room of the Crocker cousin: that trusted guy, who worked so hard. San Francisco society was all gathered there, to witness this on the night of the Cotillion.

Lise walked, coughing outside to the curb and leaned against Kyle's Packard, breathing in the fresh air. She staggered and steadied herself, hand on the hood. Kyle lurched to the car, clutching the will in his hand.

Lise looked at him, covered in blood, piss and vomit. "I'll be leaving the St. Francis," he sputtered. "Moving to the Nob. Apparently I've inherited a gold mine."

His gamble had paid off.

Lise looked into his blue eyes.

At least I know he's not a climber.

The St. Francis Hotel was begun by the trustees of the estate of Charles Crocker, one of "The Big Four" railroad magnates who had built the western portion of the transcontinental railway. o The hotel opened on March 21, 1904, and, along with the older Palace Hotel on Market Street, immediately became one of the city's most prestigious addresses.

The St. Francis Hotel soon after its opening in 1904
Source: Wikipeida

The San Francisco earthquake of 1906 badly frightened the guests, but did no structural damage to the hotel. The earthquake lasted 55 seconds. A hotel page described the pandemonium inside the hotel: "I found the floor crowded with screaming guests running every which way. As the elevators were all out of order the guests headed for the marble stairs, which were broken and cracked and falling below." Later in the morning, opera singer Enrico Caruso and Alfred Hertz, the conductor of the San Francisco Symphony, who was hosting a tour by Caruso, who were both staying at the nearby Palace Hotel, fled the Palace and came to the St. Francis, where the restaurant was still open for breakfast. Caruso carried with him a signed photograph of President Theodore Roosevelt, and swore he would never return to San Francisco; he never did.

The earthquake did not cause major structural damage to the hotel, but it did begin a series of fires along the waterfront which began to sweep west across the city. It also broke the water mains, so firemen were unable to fight the fires. An hour after midnight the fire reached Union Square and gutted the hotel.

Authenticity

Ann Eichenmuller

Tattoos are not about who we are but where we are. And that can change.

Maybe that's why God gave us so much skin. These are four-thirty thoughts as I run the damp rag over the pocked surface of the bar. If I ever kill myself, it will be on a Monday like this one, last night's game replaying silently over my head, pouring another Jack and coke for old men with nicotine-stained fingers and nowhere else to be. Last call might be the saddest time of day for drunks, but the dead hours of late afternoon are the worst for the bartender. Every face slouched on a stool is a mirror, with no music or laughter to drown the ghost of who I might have been.

The bell on the door jingles, and three people step in. Two women, a man. They blink in the dim light, held motionless for a moment by the smoke and the quiet. Then one of the women squeals, and it puts me in mind of a dog I saw lose his leg to a gator.

"Isn't this just so *authentic*?"

Ralph, a regular who coincidentally also lost his leg (though his was to a grenade in Vietnam) pushes his glass forward and rolls his eyes at me. I keep my expression carefully neutral, because a customer's a customer, and there's a stack of bills sitting in the back room that all have my name on them.

"Afternoon," I say, and my voice comes out rough and gravelly from lack of use.

The man nods at me. He is looking around and unconsciously covers his expensive watch with his hand. He glances back through the dirty window at his convertible, and I watch it pull him like a magnet. He opens his mouth, but it is too late. The women have already moved toward the bar and are sliding onto stools at the far end.

"Do you have any wine?"

I think this is the woman who did not squeal, but I can't be sure. They are sisters under the skin, stretched and injected until their tight smiles and swollen lips make them surgical twins.

I reel off the names of the wines we have. It is a surprisingly good list for this kind of bar. I know because my wife likes wine, and she is the one who picked them. The man walks over slowly, his eyes still drawn to the window, calculating the distance between himself and his BMW with each step. The women are debating white versus red and he breaks in and orders a beer. The one next to him, the squealer, shoots him a hard look that he pretends not to notice. Her husband, then. Men only ignore the women they marry.

The women fall back into their discussion, eventually settling on two Sauvignon Blancs. I learn that the squealer's name is Cynthia, and the other woman is Carleen. Neither one calls the man by name.

I pour the drinks and slide menus in front of them. Ginny has just come from the kitchen, and I tilt my head so she knows they are hers. The man looks down at my arm.

"Marine?" he asks.

He has seen the initials, nearly lost now between the brighter work, the Corvette and the wedding rings and my daughter's face, etched in pink and forever young. I nod.

"Semper Fi," he says, raising his glass.

"Hoo-rah," I answer, because he expects it, and then I step back and let Ginny slide in front of me. She needs the tips.

The screen has changed, and they look above her, though even without the distraction they would not have noticed her. Ginny is the kind of woman they would not see. She wears a shapeless navy sweater and black stretch pants that give an impression of soft heaviness. That same heaviness draws her pale face downward, and even her dark ponytail seems weighted and too much of a burden to carry.

"Are y'all eatin' or just here for a drink?" she asks. She has a hopeful voice, like a child.

I see the women exchange a glance. The man says they may get an appetizer, they're not sure.

"The smoked mullet's real good," Ginny says helpfully. "It's my favorite."

The man thanks her, and she turns away. Cynthia stifles a laugh. She pulls a cell phone from her purse and holds it up as she and Carleen press their heads together. There is a flash and more laughter, and then Cynthia turns her camera on the bar. Another flash captures all of us without asking. Ralph snorts and turns away, but Ginny looks out the window, washing glasses methodically, her eyes far away.

They finally open their menus, and Cynthia reads off the starters in an exaggerated southern drawl. They all laugh, and she goes on to the sandwiches and entrees until the joke is cold. Then she calls to Ginny sharply.

"Miss! We're ready to order!"

The squealer orders for everyone – two gator bites, one wings, blue cheese and ranch. Halfway through, she notices the gold Birthday Girl button that Ginny wears on her chest. One of the regulars gave it to her. He meant it as a joke, but Ginny had me pin it on her and wears it

like a Homecoming corsage.

"Is it your birthday?" Carleen asks, and all three focus on the button with mild amusement.

"Yes ma'am. I'm 42 today."

The woman covers it quickly, but I see her surprise. "Congratulations."

"Thank you. Did y'all want celery sticks with that?"

When Ginny goes back to the kitchen with the order, there is a flurry of conversation. They keep their voices low, but I already know what they are saying. From a distance, the women at the bar look no more than forty themselves—less if you only saw them from behind. They are congratulating themselves on their good genes and their doctor's skill that have saved them from looking like Ginny.

I pour myself four fingers of bourbon and pull this week's bar order from behind the register. I take a stool in the no man's land between Ralph and the tourists just about the time Ginny comes back with silverware and napkins. Cynthia thanks her effusively, looking at the waitress the way those Animal Welfare League ladies look at stray cats.

"That's such an unusual tattoo," she coos. "It's so detailed."

I wince at the saccharine tone, but Ginny beams at her. "It was an anniversary present from my husband. We drove all the way to Miami last month for it, to that place you see on the T.V. *Inflicting Ink*. It took the artist four hours to do."

Ginny pulls her sweater off her shoulder as Cynthia and Carleen lean forward. Delicate black stems and fragile leaves grow from the soft white mound of her breast, climbing over her collar bone and reaching up the curve of her neck. The sensuous shapes of orchids tip the stems, outlined in black and all but two empty of color. Those two are spaced some five or six inches apart, and they are wet and red like a lover's kiss.

"Didn't it hurt?"

"Some places did. The guy told me it would, because of where I wanted it—close to the bone." The trio is digesting this when a bell rings from the kitchen. "Your order's up. I'll be right back."

Cynthia turns to her husband. "Isn't that amazing? Where else could you see something like that?" She glances down at her cell phone, and I see she is itching to post about the Birthday Girl and her tattoo.

The kitchen door opens and steam coils upward through the cigarette smoke. Ginny lines the plates in front of them on the bar.

"Anything else you need?"

I look down at the liquor order. I know the question

is coming. I can taste it like a bad dream.

It is the man who asks.

"Why did you color in just two flowers?"

Ginny angles herself so that she can see her own throat in the mirror. She points to the lower flower.

"Well, this one here is for my brother Denny. He was a meth addict, and he died last summer of an overdose."

The man looks away uncomfortably while the women murmur their sympathies.

"This other one, that's for the hurricane."

There is a kind of relief on the man's face, and he grabs at this new topic like a life ring.

"Oh, yeah. You got some of the worst of it here, didn't you? Almost as bad as the Keys? I think I heard you had wind gusts up to 130 miles per hour."

"Did you have much damage?" his wife asks.

"Tree fell on the trailer, went right through the kids' bedroom," Ginny answers.

"Oh, my!" Carleen exclaims. "Was anyone hurt?"

"No, we weren't there. We stayed here."

"Here?" the woman glances around her. "You mean, in this bar?"

"Yes ma'am. For thirteen days. Me, my husband, our three kids, along with Pete over there," Ginny gestures at me, "his wife, their five kids, and all four of the dogs. We had a generator and plenty of food and a shotgun."

"A shotgun? What for?" the man asks.

She squints at him, uncertain if he is joking, decides he is not. "We had to protect the liquor. You know how people get when they think there's something they can get for nothin', and then where'd we be? And it's a good thing."

"You mean to say someone tried to break in?" the squealer's friend asks.

"Sure did."

I close my eyes.

It was the sixth night. We lay crowded together on mattresses lined up against the back wall. I had shut off the generator around eleven to save gas and everyone had gone to bed, but with the air off the sheets were damp with the September heat, and all I could smell was sweat and old grease. I stared up at the ceiling I couldn't see for an hour or more, worrying about the twelve mouths in this room who depended the bar to feed them, and the mortgage money I wouldn't have if the power didn't come on soon. I guess I finally just passed out, and so I didn't hear them until they were already in the room.

"They got in by the side door, the one with the porch," Ginny is explaining. "It's the only one that wasn't boarded up 'cause that's where we had the generator. We were givin' it a rest, and I guess those boys just thought they'd died and gone to heaven, findin' a door unlocked on a bar."

"How many were there?" the man asks. He and the squealer and her friend have not touched their food. They are staring at Ginny, mesmerized.

"Two. They came in real quiet, and even the dogs didn't hear 'em, though I couldn't fault 'em for that. You been pestered day in and day out by eight kids with nothin' better to do, you take your rest where you kin get it. I don't know why—I didn't hear them, I was in the middle of a dream, but like I told my husband, I kinda just felt them, and I woke right up."

The door was wide open, leaving a shaft of moonlight streaming in. For a minute I saw their shapes, silhouetted against the light, and then they moved and the beam caught the raised shotgun. They saw the reflection—I heard one of them mutter a curse—and the man closest to the door turned as if to run away, but the other man kept coming.

It happened fast. It always does. But in those few seconds I saw Ginny's face in the moonlight, terrible and beautiful, like all soldiers.

"What happened?" Carleen and Cynthia breathe the question in the same moment.

Ginny shrugs.

"I shot 'em. One got away, but the other one   he got kilt. That flower's for him. Can I get y'all anything else?"

The three sit in stunned silence. The man finally chokes out a "No, thank you," and Ginny turns her back on them and begins drying the clean glasses in the dishrack. I reach behind the bar and grab the remote, turning up the sound of the game.

The tourists eat quickly, without conversation, only looking up from their plates to dart glances at Ginny's back while she works. They start when Ginny turns and asks if they want another drink, and they shake their heads in unison. She puts the check in front of the man, then takes their empty plates back to the kitchen. The man pulls a stack of bills from his wallet and drops them on the bar, and the three head for the door without meeting my eyes. I watch through the window as they pile into the car, mouths and arms and hands flapping like puppets brought to life.

"How do you like that!"

It is Ginny, shaking her head in amazement, holding up the check and the bills. "Ninety dollars for a thirty-nine-dollar check!"

She opens the register, smiling, and as she leans forward the two dead men's orchids along her neck lose their softness, squeezed into thin lines of black and red.

She does not understand. Fifty-one dollars is a small price to pay… for authenticity.

Desert Heat

Susan Williamson

The heat was incessant. A dust storm had blown out of the desert and coated my house and my sweat with gritty sand. My servant and I swept out the main rooms and finally the roof. I asked her to carry water for my bath to the rooftop tub, hoping the evening might bring a cooling breeze.

The children whined and fussed. I finally got them to eat some dates and go to bed.

At long last I climbed to the roof for a refreshing soak. The full moon shone down, reflected in the clear water. A small breeze stirred the palms below. I uncovered my head and shook out my gritty hair before dropping my dirty robes on the roof. I stretched, admiring my firm breasts and rounded contours. I could hear music coming from somewhere in the palace. Was the king playing his harp?

God, I missed Uriah. The war was pointless and had been going on forever. I stepped into the tub and sank down until only my face was above the surface. I leaned back to wet my hair and began to wave it through the water. The music grew louder. I washed in time with the music. The rough cloth aroused me as I rubbed. I rubbed harder, thinking about Uriah.

My family had thought him a good catch—a mighty soldier, a man of valor. But what good was a man if he was always gone? True, we had a nice enough house, in sight of the palace. I had servants and plenty of food and drink. But a woman had needs.

David never went off to war anymore. I thought about the women in the palace. There were so many of them. I giggled. Was there a schedule? Or did he play favorites? What if you were his favorite? He was so hot. That ruddy complexion, the way his robes draped over his fine body made me tingle just looking at him. And, to walk with the king--think of the peasants groveling and bowing--that would be a total kick. I fanaticized for a few minutes.

I sighed and stood up, stretching again, luxuriating in the freedom of my naked body in the jasmine-scented air. I stepped out of the tub and swayed to the music before picking up my clean robe.

The music stopped. Almost unconsciously, I turned toward the palace. There was a man, in shadow, watching me from a parapet.

I froze. Then I turned away and slowly draped my robe over my body and shook out my wet hair. I made every move deliberate. I hoped he had gotten a good show for his effort. Who was he? Surely, not the king. He would be busy with a wife or concubine.

I climbed down into the house and checked on the children. They slept quietly. Relaxed from my bath and tired from my day, I eased to my sleeping mat. I dreamed about Uriah. I could see him across a chasm, calling my name. But neither of us could get closer.

The morning dawned slightly cooler. I gathered rice and lamb from the market and dates from our trees. A messenger from the palace waited outside my door.

"The king requests your presence," he said.

"What?" I thought about last night and felt the blush creeping up my face. "When?"

"This evening, when you have finished your dinner. Come to the south gate and he will meet you there."

He didn't wait for an answer, but turned and walked briskly back toward the palace.

Guilt engulfed me. Had I really danced naked before the king? I tried to rationalize. I hadn't known anyone was watching. He shouldn't have been looking.

I should send a message. "My time of impurity has come today." Or "I will be true to my husband. I am flattered, o noble King, but I am a woman of virtue." I fumbled through my chores, clumsy and distracted.

I was unlikely to see Uriah for many months. Who would ever know? David wouldn't tell him. In the end I sent no message. At full dark I dressed in my best robe. The children and servants were sound asleep.

I crept out the door and walked quickly to the palace, pulling my cloak over my face. I was trembling all over. What if he had second thoughts? What if a guard found me at the gate and asked my business? I almost turned back. But lust moved me forward.

He stood in the shadows and reached for my hand.

"You are so beautiful, Bathsheba. I wasn't sure you would come, but I am so glad you did. I have admired you for many years. Come let us have some wine."

Maybe we would only talk and become friends. I knew that was a ridiculous thought. I felt magic when I touched his hand. We went into a small parlor and he seated me on a couch covered in soft sheepskins. Musky incense burned in the corner. He poured wine for me and placed it in my hand before pouring his own. He gently pulled back my cloak and loosed my hair. He ran his fingers through it while he sat beside me.

We talked about the scent of the desert, our favorite flowers, growing up on the plains. Soon we were kissing, and there was no turning back.

He sent for me several times, although not every night. My guilt grew alongside my passion. I counted the days. It was time for my impurity to come, but it did not. I hesitated—so I was late, so what? A week later, he sent for me. I worried all day long. I thought about going to one of the wise women. They would have an herb to take care of things. But I would have to admit my sin. And the old women were all terrible gossips.

I went to the palace as planned. I started crying as soon as David reached for me.

"What is it, dear heart? What can be so sad?"

I told him.

He turned and walked away from me. My heart broke. Would he deny it all and let me be stoned?

He paced for a few minutes before he walked back and gently put his arm around me. "I have a solution. I will call Uriah home for a break. You will be with him, and the child will be assumed to be his."

That might be the answer.

"Go on home. I will arrange for Uriah to come within the fortnight." Could I pull it off? When Uriah came could I lie with him again as before?

I ran home and went to bed sobbing. I had to make this work.

Uriah was coming. We cleaned the house and prepared a banquet. The children made garlands of olive leaves and decorated the door for his welcome. I heard a commotion and I looked out to see him marching down the road, his relatives and friends shouting to welcome him. I ran to him and we embraced.

The servants and I readied the feast. His parents and siblings joined us, along with their families.

At dark, his father stood up. "We welcome our honorable son home from the battle, but he must rest and be with his family and so we must leave them in peace." Uriah's brothers winked and hooted with laughter.

Their departure took some time so I went to our private chamber to prepare. I loosed my hair and rubbed on perfume while I waited. And waited. The house was quiet. Where was he? I walked outside.

Uriah was spreading his bedding in the courtyard.

"What are you doing? I have made ready in our chamber."

He took his hands and held me by the shoulders. "I am here, but my men are still in the battlefield. I know not why the king has called me home, perhaps to learn more about the battle, but I cannot lie with my wife while my men languish in the plains."

What in Hades? I thought. "But Uriah, I am your wife. I have waited long for your arrival so that we could again join in our consecrated union. It is only right and your duty to lie with me."

"But, alas, as a man of honor, I cannot. I will meet with the king tomorrow and return to the battle forthwith."

Damn his man-of-honor foolishness. What now? Maybe by tomorrow night?

I tried to be civil while I served his breakfast. He smiled nobly up at me. We discussed friends and relatives and household matters. I let my hands linger on his shoulders and rub over his chest. I left my hair uncovered and swished my perfumed auburn curls by his face.

He laughed. "Stop with the seduction scene. I will be true to my men. God willing, the war will be ending soon, and I can come home to be your husband." With that, he left for the palace.

He returned an hour later and filled his pack with provisions. "I'm off to battle again, my love." He gave me a chaste kiss on the cheek and walked off into the rising sun.

Could I run away when I began to show? I tried to remember any distant cousin or aunt who might take me in, but I came up with no one.

That night, David sent for me again. He asked if we had enjoyed our reunion.

"What reunion? Your virtuous, honorable soldier refused to sleep with me while his men were still in the battlefield."

"Oh, Hades."

"Indeed. Now I'll be stoned like a common whore."

"No, love, I will find a way." He paced while I sobbed. "I will change the battle plans and send him to lead at the front. He will surely perish."

I stopped crying. I was shocked to the core. "But, David, he is a good man. You can't have him killed."

David stared at me. "I am the king. I cannot control what happens in battle, but I must order my leaders to lead. I am not responsible for what the enemy does."

I ran back to my house. What had I become?

ALEC REAM is an author and poet living in the Northern Neck of Virginia. His work has been printed in *Decanto Poetry Magazine, Western Viewpoints 2014, Poetic Images: the Great American West 2015, The Society of Classical Poets Annual Journals*, and in several issues of *The Lyric*. A member of the Demosthenian Literary Society at the University of Georgia, he deployed to Hawija. He continues to write, lecture and work for Delta Kappa Epsilon International.

ANN EICHENMULLER is the author of the non-fiction book *Writing Rx* as well as three novels: *Kind Lies, The Lies We Are*, and *The Lies Beneath*. She is an award-winning essayist and travel writer whose work has been featured in *All at Sea, Chesapeake Style, Chesapeake Bay*, and *Motorhome* magazines.

Visit her website at www.AnnEichenmuller.com.

SUSAN WILLIAMSON is a horse person, gardener, writer, and reader. She has worked as an extension agent, a newspaper editor, a community and adult education coordinator, a riding instructor, trainer, barn manager, adjunct professor, and manager of a local farm-to-table cooperative. University of Kentucky and the University of California, Davis are her alma maters. She has written a children's book, three mysteries, and two "how to" books.

It Began with a Conversation

Mary Lynn Bayliss

Readers of "The Journal" may be interested in learning how I happened to write The Dooleys of Richmond: An Irish Immigrant Family in the Old and New South which was published by the University of Virginia Press in 2017. It all began in a conversation with a lawyer and historian named Drew Carneal who was a member of the Board of Directors and chairman of the Historical Committee of the Maymont Foundation in Richmond. The foundation manages the 100 acre Maymont estate, now a museum and park owned by the city, which was left to it in 1925 by a childless couple, James Henry and Sallie May Dooley, who had lived there. Now a Virginia Historic Landmark listed on the National Register of Historic Places, Maymont's features include a Gilded Age mansion, an arboretum, Italian and Japanese Gardens. It is one of the city's treasures.

When I happened to ask Drew how things were going at Maymont, he replied that the Board was doing well raising the money needed to keep the gates open, but, despite the keen interest of the Board and tourists, very little was known about the Dooleys whose papers were ordered burned by Mrs. Dooley's relatives after her death. Before our conversation was over, I mentioned that I had some spare time and offered to do a little research if that would be helpful.

Anyone who has ever been on a committee knows what happened next. Drew sent a very nice letter inviting me to join the Historical Committee. My first task as a committee member was to make a list of the books in the mansion library for insurance purposes---to determine if there were first editions or rare books of great value on the shelves. Well, there are over 1200 books in that library, and it took me three years of Mondays to make that list. People began to tease me and ask if I were reading the books instead of listing them for the foundation files. I replied that I wasn't reading the books, I was reading the scribbles in the margins and on the front and back fly leaves and in the process learning about the Dooleys, not about just one generation, but three generations of them. Some of the things I was learning surprised me. For instance, I discovered that although wealthy enough to collect special editions, the Dooleys were readers, not collectors of books. By the time I finished that list, I was hooked. I wanted to learn more about the Dooleys. I spent the next twenty years doing just that.

In the beginning I had no idea what I would find. Little did I know that in the course of my research I would unearth information about Irish immigrants which would broaden my understanding and contradict stereotypes about them. I didn't expect to have to dig deeply into the records of the Confederate Army to complete the portrait of the James Dooley of Maymont, his brother, and his Irish immigrant father. I didn't expect to discover that James Dooley, who to this day is always called "Major Dooley," had never held that rank. It was his father, John Dooley, who had earned the rank of Major in battle. James had only been a private in the First Virginia during the Civil War and had served in the Confederate Army only briefly before being severely wounded, left on the battlefield and taken prisoner-of-war. I also discovered that after learning what had happened to James, his father had founded the Richmond Ambulance Committee, a volunteer cadre of ninety men who, at their own expense, risked their lives for the following three years of the war to bring the wounded off the battlefields while the war raged around them. Those discoveries led to a talk I gave at Maymont. Its title was: "Will the Real Major Dooley Please Stand Up."

Later I discovered that in the final days of the Civil War when Richmond's business district suffered what is called the "Evacuation Fire," John Dooley lost everything he had spent thirty years building. The manufacturing, wholesale and retail arms of his business had all gone up in flames. But that, as I knew, was not the end of the dramatic story of the family. James went on to make a fortune. He and his wife became great philanthropists whose gift of their estate to Richmond, as I later learned, was only one of their many gifts to the city and only the beginning of the story about them that I would eventually write.

NECESSARY WOMEN

Thea Marshall

Back in 1619, the very first women in any number, in this case perhaps 50, arrived in Jamestown. It was part of an effort to change the man-woman ratio. Up until then, it was practically an all male society, except for a couple of the wives who had come with their husbands.

It was an all male society, those first settlers of Virginia, who struggled desperately and ineffectually against disease, starvation, and Indian massacres. Coincidently, in the summer of the year, the first group of women arrived and the very first Virginia House of Burgesses issued this most provocative statement:

"In this newe plantation it is not knowne whether man or woman be the most necessary."

I guess I could put that into the massive group of declarations and questions about women; it might even rank up there with Freud's "What do women want?" The good Burgesses were talking about those early spinsters or maids, as they were called, who braved the voyage to Virginia to lose their spinsterhood—to whom, they did not know.

Getting back to "necessary," what was necessary in the 17th Century, and actually beyond? Well, first, the infant colony was simply trying to survive on fish and corn, but later on, more supplies arrived from England and survival was slightly less "iffy," there was grinding corn, and if they were lucky, milking cows, butchering meat, brewing beer, growing vegetables, making clothes, mending clothes, washing clothes, and hauling water. Well, it seems, according to historians, all that stuff (oh, and let's not forget emptying chamber pots) was women's work.

Now, whether we are talking about women who came from England, free or indentured, or women who came from Africa, free or indentured, it was equal opportunity to be worked to death.

And then there was women's most vital role, procreation. Without increasing the population, the colony could not survive and that is where marrying well, and often, comes in. While the "often" part was generally the purview of the men—females married young and it wasn't uncommon for a woman to be pregnant almost her entire life, giving birth to 12 or 13 children and dying while still young. And the husband would quickly remarry to have a mother for his first set of children, as well as a housekeeper and drudge in chief—and more children.

This was true of the gentry, land-poor folks, watermen, and farmers. This Northern Neck's most notable land owner and first so called millionaire, Robert King Carter, had five wives, and his descendants number in the tens of thousands.

Of course, all this took place well after 1619, when the question of who is more necessary, men or women, was posed, I don't have an answer. Instead, a "what if." What if, from the very beginning, perhaps in the *Susan Constant* or *The Discovery*, or maybe *The Godspeed*, the passenger list included as many women as men…women like Abigail Adams, Mary Wollstonecraft, Lucretia Mott, Louisa May Alcott, and Olympia Snow.

Maybe your grandmother, maybe your daughter, maybe you. And speaking of you, who are the necessary women in your lives?

Womens work in the 17th Century, carrying away the communal latrine

CHINCHILLAS!

DAD'S GET-RICH-QUICK SCHEME

Cindy L. Freeman

"If hard work were such a wonderful thing, surely the rich would have kept it all to themselves." ~ (Joseph) Lane Kirkland,

US labor union leader who served as President of the AFL-CIO for over sixteen years.

Throughout the 1950s, my dad, a dairy farmer, devised get-rich-quick schemes. His goal was to be a millionaire. He was determined to never again live through anything like the Great Depression. Many of his ideas failed to materialize. This time he had been reading in the Wall Street Journal about chinchillas, those furry rodents with highly valued pelts.

Dad researched until he found a source for purchasing several young chinchillas. Before they arrived, he set up large wire cages in the cellar and bedded them with wood shavings. Then, he ordered special food pellets formulated exclusively for chinchillas. His plan, once the creatures reached adulthood, was to sell them for their plush fur. The wood furnace in the cellar would keep the animals, whose natural habitat was Chile, toasty warm.

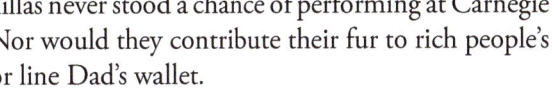

Despite Mighty Mouse being my favorite cartoon character, I was terrified of rodents and thought the animals looked no more valuable than the gray squirrels scampering about our yard.

One night, after all of us had fallen asleep, something strange happened. Piano music awakened us in the form of raggedy glissandi ascending and descending the keyboard. Since the piano was in the living room just beyond my bedroom door, Mom blamed me for the nighttime interruption.

"Lucinda," Mom called, "Stop playing the piano and go back to bed." She always used my given name when scolding me.

"It's not me!" I yelled.

"Marion?"

"Not me!" my sister shouted from her room at the opposite end of the house.

"Well, whoever it is, go to bed."

The ill-defined duet continued. After listening to a few minutes of passages in a decidedly impressionistic style, Dad was compelled to get up and check it out.

You guessed it. Two of Dad's chinchillas had escaped the cellar and were presenting their concert debut in our living room. As soon as I realized the rodents were loose, I got up, slammed my bedroom door, and cowered under the covers.

From his exasperated moaning and groaning, I could tell that Dad, who had to get up before 5:00 a.m., was not amused to have his sleep interrupted, but soon I heard him and Mom laughing amid scuffling and bumping sounds, followed by a few loud Stravinsky-type, atonal clusters (i.e. banging and crashing) on the piano. That night, we learned the hard way that, unlike squirrels, chinchillas were nocturnal.

Eventually, Mom and Dad corralled the perpetrators and returned them to their cages in the cellar. The house grew quiet again, but not before a Walton-family exchange of "good nights," along with Dad's heavy sighs and a few giggles. I have no idea how the critters escaped in the first place or what Dad did to prevent another breakout.

Weeks later, Dad's scheme ended abruptly when a chimney fire caused the cellar to fill with smoke. The chinchillas never stood a chance of performing at Carnegie Hall. Nor would they contribute their fur to rich people's coats or line Dad's wallet.

Sage-ing not Age-ing

Betty Mayo

Jeanne Johansen

Sage-ing looks at aging as a spiritual practice that involves life review and repair, harvesting wisdom from life's lessons and transmitting a legacy to future generations. With a confidence born from harvesting and a humility that sees service as the natural result of continued inner growth, we find ways to serve every day. This generosity of spirit elicits joy in human relations, while positively benefiting the families, communities and cultures we serve.

Some of Betty's Belt Buckle Awards

Barrel racing is a rodeo *event in which a* horse *and rider attempt to complete a cloverleaf pattern around preset* barrels *in the fastest time. It combines the horse's athletic ability and the horsemanship skills of a rider in order to safely and successfully maneuver a horse in a pattern around three barrels placed in a triangle in the center of an arena.*

Betty Mayo has always been horse crazy. "My first word was 'pony', and I knew I wanted one from the time I could say the word."

She was born in Carroll County in the southwestern part of the Commonwealth of Virginia. One fifth of the county lies in the Virginia Piedmont region; the rest is part of the Blue Ridge Mountains a segment of the Appalachian Mountains. "My mother, Mary Ethel Smith Beamon, was from the mountains, and my daddy, William Earl Beamon, was from Portsmouth on a construction project. They both worked, so in the summer I would stay with my aunt and uncle on their farm. That's where I started working with horses. I would help on the farm all day and ride at night. I was never too tired to ride. I loved the garden and the mountains."

Their neighbor had a tall sawhorse, and Betty bought it from him when she was 10 years old. She put a saddle on it, and she would practice balancing and riding the wobbly trestle.

Her father moved the family to Hampton where he became the head rigger for NASA Langley. "I had a collection of little horses in my room, and my brain was obsessed with horses and I about wore my daddy down."

When it was time to give birth to Betty, her mother would return to her grandmother's home in Hillsville, Virginia. Her father stayed in Hampton by himself. "That's the way mountain people did it. No hospital. They did what they trusted with people who knew the old ways. When it was my time to give birth to my baby girl, I had to out do her. So, I had my baby girl in the car."

At one point, her father promised her a goat. "I would have settled for a goat," she said. "But, fortunately the goat was sold. So, on I went until my daddy finally agreed to look for a pony."

"Down on the end of the street where we lived, a lady had a chicken field. I used the field, and my daddy built me a stall on skids and drug it to the field for my new pony. He also built me a bridge across the marsh in back of our house."

When she was 12, her father went to a sale in Suffolk. The auctioneer demonstrated the gentleness of one pony by crossing under its belly. "That's the one my daddy bought for me. It was a dark brown and white pinto with a black mane and tail. I named him Pretty Boy."

Betty jumping on Zsa-Zsa Gabor

Horse Manure

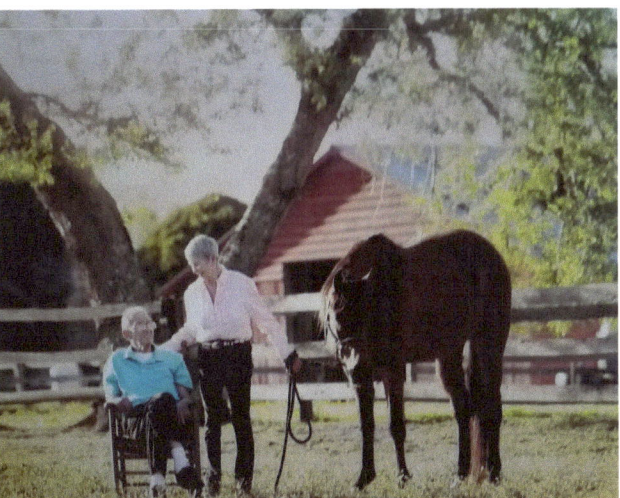

It was horse manure that first got her attention, when Betty and future husband Mike were seventh graders at Buckroe Junior High School in Hampton. He made certain she heard a conversation between him and another boy where Mike talked about shoveling horse manure.

That was it. "It was just like love at first sight," she says. "We decided to get married when we got out of school and have a horse farm."

Betty and Mike married right after high school. She found a house for sale on Sinclair Road in Hampton. There was a big field next door where they would be allowed to keep horses. Since they were too young to sign for a loan themselves, Betty's parents took out a mortgage on their new home, transferring the deed into their names as soon as they were of age. They both got jobs, and they worked hard.

"We were able to get a pony and pony cart when we hadn't been married three months. We didn't do anything for 10 years but pay the bills and play with the horses. Zsa-Zsa and Fifi, two 6-month-old fillies, had come to live with the pony. I was English riding at the time. Then, I watched the barrel racers. I told Mike that I wanted to do that. He sold his show saddle and bought two barrel racing saddles so we could both race. And I was serious. Before long, barrel racing became a part of my life."

Their children were born in 1958 and 1964.

When Betty was growing up in the early 1950s, she could ride horseback from East Hampton to Buckroe Beach to Grandview Beach, then all the way back through Fox Hill. "We would leave early in the morning and come back at night. But the city grew and the trails I used to ride were gone. So, we moved to rural Gloucester in 1976. Mike had to get up at 4:30 a.m. to commute to work at Pembroke Construction Co. in Hampton. My husband made our dreams come true." Her husband, Russell Glenn "Mike" "Tight Mike" Mayo Jr. passed away on May 19, 2017.

Barrel Racing

In November 1996 Betty won her first world

barrel-racing title in Augusta, Georgia. There were 150 contestants in the competition, and she became the 1996 senior reserve champion at the National Barrel Horse Association competition.

Betty qualified for the world finals many times. To qualify for this award, you must earn NBHA points at sanctioned shows throughout the competition year. The exact number of World Championship qualifiers is determined by the outcome of competition in each competition district. In 2017, she competed in the NBHA National Colonials, winning first place in the senior 3rd division on *Ruby's A Dream*. Her time was 16.464 seconds. She brought her silver belt buckle to our aerobics class to show it off, the same class where so many of us have recuperated from major injuries.

Injuries

Betty has had her fair share of injuries. "I have hit the ground so many times. I have had a broken ankle, foot, knee, elbow and shoulder (twice), and dislocated a collarbone. I've got a steel plate and six screws in this left shoulder from a horse falling on me in 1991."

Of course, that doesn't include the "little ones" like cracked ribs or fractured teeth.

Despite these small annoyances, she is at the Riverside

Wellness Center in Gloucester, Virginia every morning for water aerobics. That's where I first met her, and she has been my inspiration ever since.

We had a conversation in September, 2017. It was the day she brought in her silver belt buckle she had won at the NBHA Nationals.

Our water aerobics class was over, and I was sulking in the deep end of the pool. I felt like my progress had stalled.

"As long as you keep these muscles working, you'll have them," she said.

Please, just leave me alone. Like I said, I was sulking.

"I lost my husband in May," she said.

"I'm sorry to hear that," was all I could manage.

"I didn't think I should compete this year. Only three months since my husband passed."

At the time Betty Mayo was 80 years old. And still barrel racing, winning, getting up after falling down...and willing to watch over me.

Betty was born on September 28, 1937. Today, at the age of 82, she still has a love for horses and enjoys riding every day.

Artist

In addition to her many awards in barrel-racing, Betty

is also an artist. Her paintings include her horses, and a special one of her nephew who was a jockey. "You didn't have to be short to be a jockey. It was the weight that mattered. Once he weighed more than 114 pounds, he had to quit as a jockey, and he became the track steward. But I captured him on one of his horses."

Betty Mayo is a sage and has those qualities that define one:

- Deep Listening
- Compassion
- Joyfulness
- Peacefulness
- Open Communication
- Lifelong Learning
- Inclusiveness
- Integrity
- Reverence for Life
- Respect

Betty's Advice for a Happy Life

- Serve the Lord

- Stick with your family

- Stay busy doing something

- Whatever your heart says, do it

- Go outside

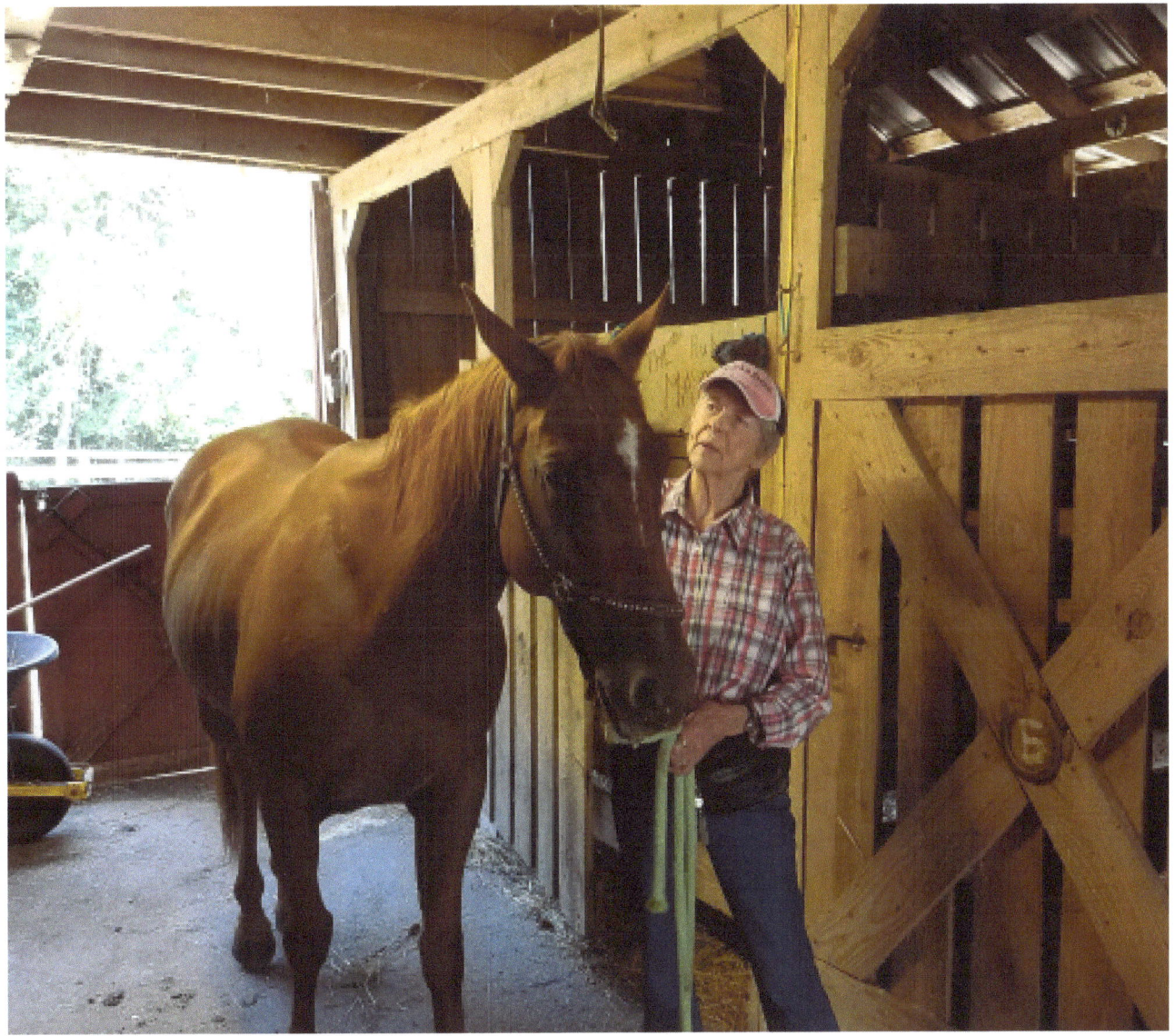

Betty and her new horse Jetty (Registered Name: Rey Wimpy Jean)

A Lesson in Generosity

Gwen Keane

My parents divorced when I was four years old. I was a very loved and spoiled only child, who escaped the scars often caused by a divorce. Love conquered my insecurities, and thus I learned life values---especially those found in a rural community, like the Northern Neck, where people matter.

My father's parents, Grandma and Granddaddy raised me. My other Grandparents, Grandma Sue and Grandpa Ted, owned a printing business on F and 9th Streets in Washington, D.C. Grandpa Ted ran the printing press, while Grandma Sue, the CEO, solicited classified printing jobs from the Department of Defense.

My visits to Washington, D.C. were always memorable. I would go to work with my grandparents and accompany Grandma Sue to the Pentagon, where she met with government officials. I would always be introduced as her granddaughter "Doodlebug." Those trips to the Pentagon seemed to last all day, yet I was content to sit in the cafeteria eating hot donuts and french fries while the adults talked. Grandma Sue, quite the dresser, wore fancy clothes. During my visits, each morning I sat next to her on the vanity bench, in front of her dressing table, absorbing each step of her makeup ritual. She would begin by cleaning her face with Ponds facial cream. Next she put on her Merle Norman facial foundation, then eye makeup and face powder that she applied with a powder puff. In place of a brush, she would use her little finger to apply her bright red lipstick. Her ritual concluded after she placed several drops of *Tweed* perfume behind each ear. *Tweed* was as important to Grandma Sue as her *Jack Daniels* whiskey.

After I became an adult, I often thought about that perfume. I, like Grandma Sue, shopped at Woodword and Lothrop, in D.C., but I never found her *Tweed* perfume. Ten years ago, while looking through a Vermont Store catalog, I finally found it. I became so thrilled to have my very own bottle but the thrill didn't last long.

For some reason, the bottle of perfume didn't smell like I had remembered it. But today I still possess that bottle of *Tweed* that sits unused on a shelf in my bathroom. Grandma Sue wore a show-stopper outfit each day. I remember her owning a navy blue crepe sheath with colored rhinestones, designed to look like a long stemmed flower, which encompassed the entire right front side of the dress. She would wear navy blue sheer stockings, dyed satin shoes and carry a large matching purse. I became enamored with her wardrobe.

At home in Ditchley, I had been used to seeing Grandma in handmade cotton skirts and white blouses. Her wardrobe had been sparse, yet practical. On Sundays when we attended church, she either wore her only suit, a basic navy blue, or one of the few tailored dresses she owned. Grandma's appearance complimented her personality, a strong-minded person who didn't make a fuss about clothes. Grandma Sue, however, always looked as if she had stepped from a fashion magazine. She appeared vibrant, swanky and sexy.

Grandma Sue, a very heavy set woman, had been a well-known customer at the Lane Bryant Store on F Street in Washington, D.C. She once asked me to help her select a leather purse. Enthusiastically I removed purses from all the shelves within my reach and showed them to her, only to have them rejected. Later she said, "Now Doodlebug, I need a purse big enough to hold all of my important things, including my pint of *Jack Daniels*." It was then I began to believe all grandmothers who lived in the big city carried large purses with a pint of *Jack Daniels*.

During my visits in the summer, our Saturdays were spent at the Rosecroft Raceway in Maryland. We would sit in front of the big picture window in the air-conditioned clubhouse that overlooked the raceway and the crowd of people sitting on the bleachers outside. Grandma Sue would bet on the horses I selected. During the races, she had the tenacity to turn away from me and open her purse. I assumed she was taking out money to put on the next bet. My favorite number was three, and after I tired of shouting "Come on Fe" I would begin to whine and ask, "When can we visit the horses?"

Skipping toward the stables, but always looking back, I'd soon find myself standing in front of a horse stall, where I waited for my grandparents. Once Grandma Sue took a hard fall, that resulted in her rolling around on the soft ground. Laughing loudly, I said, "Big fat cow falls down." Neither of my grandparents acknowledged my rude remark.

I was adored by both sets of grandparents, and like all grandchildren, I enjoyed being spoiled. Grandma Sue and Grandpa Ted frequently visited me in Ditchley. Whenever Grandma got the telephone call that my other grandparents were coming for the weekend, we all got busy making sure the guest bedroom was presentable, the grass was cut, and there was plenty of food in the house. Finally, after they arrived Grandma Sue would exit the Ford station wagon carrying many packages and her large purse. Grandpa Ted always seemed to be left behind to struggle with the luggage, that eventually he carried upstairs to the bedroom.

After giving and receiving hugs, Grandma and I would be invited to gather around the bed to watch Grandma Sue unpack. She always arrived with special gifts for both of us.

"Emily, I thought this dress would look nice on you. So, go ahead and try it on. Let's see how it fits."

Grandma, not wanting to offend Grandma Sue, would take the dress and disappear into a bedroom. Later she returned wearing it, and whether it looked good or not, Grandma Sue's comment would always be the same, "The dress looks perfect." Grandma Sue brought other gifts, like stockings and underwear. Once when she arrived with an abundance of packages, she instructed Grandpa Ted to take them directly to the kitchen and put them on the table for Grandma to open. She had given Grandma a complete set of *Revere Ware* pans with copper bottoms. Grandma Sue had thought these new pans would replace Grandma's dented aluminum pans. When the weekend had ended, Grandma stored the new pans under the counter and brought them out for only special occasions—a visit from Grandma Sue and Grandpa Ted.

When it came to managing money, my grandmothers were complete opposites, yet both were generous individuals. During a Thanksgiving visit, Grandma Sue asked if we had any neighbors in need of food. Grandma spoke about a family on Route 200 who lived in an old farmhouse that looked as if it were falling down. She had seen the children standing at the end of the lane in cold weather without coats as they waited for the school bus. Grandma Sue reached into her big purse and took out her checkbook. Two days before Christmas we went grocery shopping. We got home late and Grandma instructed me to leave the groceries in the car. It had gotten dark by the time we finished supper. Grandma, who had left the kitchen before removing the dishes from the table, returned wearing her coat and holding her purse.

"Baby, get your coat. We've got an errand to take care of." I knew when to ask questions and this was not one of those times. We got in the car and Grandma turned on the headlights, as we headed toward Route 200. We hadn't travelled far, when Grandma slowed down the car, and turned into a dirt lane. Our car lights shined on the house in the distance and the window with a lighted candle.

After we arrived in front of the house, Grandma cut the car lights and engine off and instructed me to not get out. We had a full moon that night, and sitting there cold, I watched Grandma lift the bags of groceries and set them down just inside the screenless porch door. No words had been spoken.

I understood what she had done, but I didn't understand why she had chosen to handle it that way.

So, I asked, "Grandma, why didn't you knock on the door? You know someone was home because of the burning candle in the window."

"No one wants others to know when they are down on their luck. It's just best we perform our deeds in silence."

I never forgot that night, and often I have wondered how that family felt, finding bags of groceries left on their porch by strangers.

NEARLY IDYLLIC
CALM IN THE STORM

David Cariens

I arrived six months before Pearl Harbor; my formative years spent in a cocoon of warmth and love. Indeed, my early life was wonderful, a life largely, but not completely sheltered from the world around me; a world gone mad; a world of unspeakable atrocities—horrors on a magnitude hard to fathom even today.

Perhaps the madness dawning on my young consciousness was a harbinger of what lay ahead for me. In my case, it would be madness and fanaticism, on a much, much smaller scale than was taking place in the world I was awakening to. It was, nevertheless, devastating.

The madness would come in many forms—the destruction of the loving family I was raised in, threats on my life as well as the lives of my wife and children, and finally, the murder of the mother of my oldest grandchild.

Over 70 years ago, as I became conscious of the world around me I did not understand the distant barbarity, but some of my earliest memories are trying to reconcile the affection and security of my life with what I heard my parents talking about in hushed tones. I was, after all, only three or four when I became aware that millions of people were being slaughtered simply because they were not part of the master race. The tragedies unfolding in Europe and in the Far East were far removed from my loving idyllic existence.

When Mom and Dad took us to the movies, there was always a newsreel. Those short films were part of the program in every movie theater's playbill. Sometimes the newsreels contained vignettes about beautiful movie stars, a fashion show, or a short human-interest story. But always there was the war. Dead bodies, streets in ruin, people scavenging for food—a hellish existence. And always the same questioning faces looking at the audience, "Why me, why this pain, why this suffering?"

I looked at children's dirty, gaunt faces and wondered, *are they like me? Why isn't that me? What are their names? Why am I different, why am I not going through what they are experiencing?*

At the end of the movie, we left the darkness, squinting as our eyes adjusted to the bright lights of the theater lobby. We made our way to the car and back to our comfortable home, warm beds, and no worries about where our next meal would come from.

After the war ended, newsreels and pictures in magazines were horrific, showing the concentration camp liberations. Again, there were pictures of children my age—with ribs protruding under the gaunt, stretched skin of their chests. There were emaciated bodies of men and women being set free from Hitler's camps—dazed by the world outside and their new-found freedom.

Children sit among the rubble of their home September 1940

What did they do to deserve such a fate? The answer? *Nothing.*

Soldiers began returning home; rationing was lifted, moods improved; all the while the revelations of horror grew.

Reports of the millions who had perished were hard to fathom, particularly for a young child: people who had been shot, hanged, or gassed. They committed no crimes; they were simply not part of Hitler's master race. *What* did it mean to be a Jew, a Slav, or a gypsy? Why did the Germans and others hate them so much they would try to annihilate them? Why did they or any group of people deserve extermination?

I would spend much of my adult life trying to find answers to those questions. But to this day I have no answer to why hate is so deeply ingrained in human nature.

Schadenfreude

I simply know hate and its handmaidens, ridicule, sarcasm, jealousy, belittling humor, and bullying are centuries-old, despicable characteristics of human behavior. Hate is a basic ingredient of mankind's madness—it is the fountain from which the others flow. Hate seems to be an indelible part of our nature; hate is part of our madness. Fittingly, the Germans have a word for wallowing in hate and enjoying the misfortunes of others—*schadenfreude*.

My idyllic progression from birth to manhood would periodically be shattered by hate as its acolytes surfaced in my family. A form of the unbridled hatred I saw, heard and later read about and in school would destroy the family I loved so very much.

In 1826 American writer William Hazlitt wrote *The Pleasure of Hating.* He asserts:

"The pleasure of hating, like a poisonous mineral, eats into the heart of religion, and turns it to rankling spleen and bigotry; it makes patriotism an excuse for carrying fire, pestilence, and famine into other lands: it leaves to virtue nothing but the spirit of censoriousness, and a narrow, jealous, inquisitorial watchfulness over the actions and motives of others."

Hazlitt's words struck me deeply following the recent death of a close friend's daughter. In high school, that daughter was subjected to intense ridicule because of her appearance and because she was Jewish. Her classmates teased her, mocked her and gave her a name—*The Frog*. It stuck. The damage was done.

A couple of years before her death at age 69, she asked her only grandchild to call her *Nana Frog*. A talented and tormented woman, she fought many demons and never recovered from the hate, the bullying, and the ridicule she endured. Her family gave me a copy of her poem.

As a small child, I felt the warmth of love. Nevertheless, I had trouble going to sleep. I lay awake at night after seeing pictures of soldiers—dead and wounded. My parents left the hall light on to help me go to sleep, but the resulting shadows frequently turned into grotesque villains or monsters. More than once I awoke screaming, mistaking the clothes rack in the corner of my bedroom for a shadowy Nazi bent on killing me.

At that early age I kept going back to the same questions: *How does all of the pain and killing fit into the love and forgiveness I hear on Sunday mornings; where were the fundamental decencies such as respect for human life? What about 'thou shalt not kill?"*

I wonder this even more today when churches here in the Northern Neck of Virginia remain silent as anti-Semites march in Charlottesville shouting, "Jews will not replace us." I am perplexed at why leaders of those congregations, with few exception, are mute when innocent worshipers in Pittsburgh and San Diego synagogues are gunned down. I hang my head when people of 'faith' are largely silent when a white supremacist massacres African-American worshipers during prayers at a Charleston church.

I am angry when large numbers of my fellow countrymen and women say nothing as the country I love puts people fleeing oppression and violence in concentration camps, separating small children from their parents.

My childhood horrors have returned to haunt me.

Life As A Frog

Sometimes I dream
Of being a frog –
A Jewish frog in search
Of kosher bugs.
Other frogs
Wouldn't call me names
Or tell me that
I killed their god.
Even if I was
A different shade of green
I would be
Another frog.

REINCARNATION

AND OTHER PARANORMAL ELEMENTS

Mary Montague Sikes

Reincarnation is the philosophical or religious concept that the non-physical essence of a living being starts a new life in a different physical form or body after biological death. It is also called rebirth or transmigration, and is a part of the Samsara doctrine of cyclic existence. In short, Samsara is the cycle of death and rebirth. Reincarnation is a central tenet of Indian religions, namely Jainism, Buddhism, Sikhism and Hinduism, although there are Hindu groups that do not believe in reincarnation but believe in an afterlife. A belief in rebirth/metempsychosis was held by Greek historic figures, such as Pythagoras, Socrates, and Plato. It is also a common belief of various ancient and modern religions such as Spiritism, Theosophy, Anthroposophy and Eckankar and as an esoteric belief in many streams of Orthodox Judaism. It is also found (in different forms) in some beliefs of North American Natives.

As a child I remember wondering if I had lived before. Had I been reincarnated? I believed I had. My mother was appalled, but my grandmother never doubted such things.

Years later, I had déjà vu experiences, especially in the city of Vienna, Austria where I felt quite at home exploring the ancient streets. From the first moment I saw them, the buildings looked familiar to me and so did the art decorative work on their facades.

Did I have memories from the past? Is that possible? I continue to ask that question.

Books about reincarnation have always intrigued me. Reincarnation and especially Dr. Ian Stevenson's research books on the subject. Dr. Stevenson (1918 – 2007) worked for 50 years with the University of Virginia School of Medicine and served for a time as Director of Personality Studies in the Department of Psychiatry there.

"In many parts of the world, some young children, usually between the ages of two and five, speak about a previous life they claim to have lived," he noted.

Dr. Stevenson went to India and other Asian countries to research many of these cases and found instances in which actual events in a deceased person's life were remembered by a child claiming to be that person. In many of the cases, the two families had not known each other prior to Dr. Stevenson's visits. Often these children have birth marks related to a trauma in a deceased person's life, such as the wound that killed him or her. Usually children do not remember a past life by the time they reach age seven, Dr. Stevenson found.

I was surprised to read that Dr. Stevenson's wife, Dr. Margaret Pertzoff (1926-2009), who was a history professor at Randolph Macon Woman's College, did not share his paranormal views. It is interesting to learn more about his teachings by watching videos of his presentations available on the Internet.

You can find hundreds of non-fiction books about various paranormal experiences that can inspire writers. In *Hello From Heaven* by Bill and Judy Guggenheim, the authors write about after death communications (ADCs). Often in these communications, contact is made with a deceased person by a butterfly or a rainbow. These are symbols that often are used in fictional stories or in paintings.

The Guggenheims point out that *Hamlet* by William Shakespeare is based on an ADC experience. In the famous play, the young prince Hamlet is mourning the death of his father who was reported to have been bitten by a poisonous snake. His deceased father appears to him and explains that his brother, Claudius, murdered him by pouring poison in his ear while he slept. Claudius wanted to marry his widow and become the king of Denmark. His son pledges to avenge his father's death which creates the plot for the remainder of the play.

A Christmas Carol by Charles Dickens is an example of another famous story featuring an ADC. In this book, Jacob Marley who is the deceased business partner of Ebenezer Scrooge appears to warn Scrooge of what will happen if he does not change his materialistic ways and become more charitable.

Bill Guggenheim wonders if it is mere coincidence that both of these famous works contain examples of after death communications, or were the two authors familiar with examples of ADCs in their contemporary times? In that case Shakespeare and Dickens adapted these events for literary usage.

Since I first read her book, *Forever Love,* many years ago, Meg Chittenden has been one of my favorite authors. In this book, she used an amazing range of background research into the paranormal to create a compelling plot.

In 1990 Chittenden wrote another reincarnation story. In *This Time Forever* Liz Brooks, very much a business partner of Ebenezer Scrooge, appears to warn Scrooge of what will happen if he does not change his materialistic ways and become more charitable.

Her novel starts when a best-selling author goes to England to promote her new book only to have a woman appear at her hotel door claiming the book is the same as the story her sister wrote prior to her disappearance 31 years before. The author investigates the missing woman and discovers she was born the day after the woman's disappearance. This reincarnation story is amazing with twists and turns and flashbacks that keep the pages flying. That book was written in 1988, and used copies are available on Amazon. If you can get a copy, it makes a fascinating read. It sits as a keeper on my book shelves.

In 1990 Chittenden wrote another reincarnation story. In *This Time Forever* Liz Brooks is very much a contemporary woman--a travel rep with both feet firmly planted on the ground. But suddenly, she's having these weird experiences--imagining herself in the body of Jeannie Findlay, a feisty milliner, living in Edinburgh in 1888, falling in love with Robert McAndrews, a man way above Jeannie's station in life, a man whose ancestor almost destroyed her family. It was re-released in 2002 and is available from Amazon. However, for me, this book did not live up to expectations created by Chittenden's first reincarnation story.

I have always loved to travel and over the years, I've had the opportunity to visit many memorable and often exotic locations in the United States, Canada, Europe and the Caribbean. Often on these trips, my husband and I have found gorgeous and unusual hotels. Many of these hotels and the stories behind them became part of my coffee table book, *Hotels to Remember.*

One of my favorite hotels from the book is the Hotel del Coronado near San Diego, CA. Not surprisingly, one of the reasons for my fascination with this beautiful wooden structure that dates back to the late 1800s is the story of the ghost that resides there. A young woman was murdered at the hotel in 1892. Her body was found on the steps leading to the ocean, and since that time people have reported all sorts of ghost sightings, television and newspaper reporters have investigated, and a great deal of press has been given to the Del Coronado ghost. That's

Restored photochrom print of Hotel del Coronado by William Henry Jackson, c. 1900

especially true around Halloween each year.

Back in 1994, I was pleasantly surprised to discover a book by Lori Herter in the old Silhouette Shadows series called *The Willow File* that is likely based on the ghost at The Hotel Del Coronado. However, in the story, the hotel's name is changed to The Aragon. This author, like many others, appears to have been inspired by a popular and legendary tale that still attracts guests who ask to stay in or near the room where the ghost is said to appear.

***

My own fascination with reincarnation plays out in my romance novel, *Hearts Across Forever.* From my first visit to Jamaica, I was entranced with the romantic Caribbean island. I was especially drawn to the Rose Hall Mansion and to the legend of the white witch of Rose Hall. From the moment I heard the story, I knew I had to write a book in someway related to the story.

Over the years, I've found that one way to draw paranormal elements into a story is to start it out with a dream. Those who watched the popular television series, *Medium,* might remember that the program often started with a startling, frightening dream. My book begins with a startling, frightening dream that goes back to the white witch, Annie Palmer, and days in old Jamaica when she harassed and murdered the slaves who served her.

"Hooves of two powerful horses pounded the rutted roadway leading from Rose Hall Plantation toward Montego Bay. Along one side the Caribbean Sea lapped the shore with a soft murmur.

Aunt Annie spurred Raven forward, striking the sleek black stallion with vicious strokes of her riding crop. With each whack, Aimee's heart pounded harder."

Like some of the novels I've mentioned, my story moves between Kathryn, the heroine of the present, and Aimee, the heroine who lived in old Jamaica. Kathryn enters periods of self-hypnosis that take her into the past. She has other dreams of her past-life. She also meets a doctor, loosely based on Dr. Stevenson, who guides her toward the resolution of the conflict in the story. And all the while, Kathryn is discovering a new love that is not new at all.

I have another paranormal story, *Secrets by the Sea,* which features a ghost that has haunted an old house by the sea for well over 300 years. The setting is on the Caribbean island of Antigua. This book draws in some of the history of the area and includes a lost treasure related to the ghost. The ancient home features myriad tunnels, so the reader never knows if the strange happenings are ghost-related or the result of actions by one of the living characters. Many of the 20 hotels highlighted in my coffee table book have ghosts. I believe each hotel can serve as the setting for a book. So many characters live in an author's imagination. A ghost may stand in the window of the bell tower of the Vinoy and frighten away a few of the guests. A character may board a phantom train at the St. Louis Union Station hotel and travel back in time to the early days of rail travel. There are countless ways characters might stir and live again through reincarnation or other ghostly journeys.

Meg Chittenden has done this in her stories, and so have hundreds and thousands of other authors. Meg doesn't believe in reading authors whose work you enjoy and trying to be like them.

"Live your own life as fully as possible and listen to what goes on inside your own head," she says. Meg believes in growing your own writing voice by living out a wide range of experiences.

I continue loving to travel and meeting new people. Sometimes I still encounter something new that is inexplicably familiar, and I wonder why.

Is reincarnation possible? Do I want it to be?

THEA MARSHALL is a radio personality, actress, and author. Her interview radio programs were carried over NPR in New York, Washington, and Richmond. Among her credits are the lead role in Tennessee Williams' *The Milk Train Doesn't Stop Here Anymore.* She is the author of *Neck Tales*, a collection of stories about Virginia's Northern Neck.

JEANNE JOHANSEN is an award winning author and graphic artist who has the good fortune to own High Tide Publications, Inc. She fell in love with publishing *Literary Late Bloome*r manuscripts in 2010, and hasn't stopped since. A world traveller who loves a good adventure, she grew up in California and worked for many years in the healthcare industry...until she came to her senses.

GWEN KEANE was born and raised in the Northern Neck of Virginia. She has a Master's Degree from Georgetown University in Public Administration. She retired from her federal career as a civilian employee with the U.S. Navy, with ten years as the Deputy Inspector General for the Naval Sea Systems Command. She has written three books: *Swan Wait, Local Color,* and *How Cowboy Found His Forever Home.*

Visit her website at www.GwenKeane.com

DR. MARY LYNN BAYLISS is a biographer, lecturer, and book reviewer with homes in Goochland County and Deltaville, Virginia. Her book *The Dooleys Of Richmond: An Irish Immigrant Family In The Old And New South* was a finalist in the 2018 Library of Virginia Nonfiction People's Choice Award. Dr. Bayliss has published work in *Virginia Cavalcade, The Richmond Times-Dispatch, The Dictionary Of Virginia Biography* and *Encyclopedia Virginia.*

DAVID CARIENS is a retired CIA political analyst. He wrote finished intelligence for all levels of consumers including the president and members of the intelligence and policymaking communities. Cariens continues to teach intelligence and crime analysis. He is a victims' rights advocate and the author of *A Question of Accountability: The Murder of Angela Dales* about the Appalachian School of Law in Grundy, Virginia, and V*irginia Tech: Make Sure It Doesn't Get Out*, an analysis of that rampage.

Visit his website: www. DaveCariens.com.

CINDY L. FREEMAN is author of three novels: *Unrevealed, The Dark Room,* and *I Want to Go Home,* a novella, *Diary in the Attic,* and three award-winning short stories. She began writing fiction after a forty-five-year career in music education and music ministry. Currently, she is finishing her childhood memoir about growing up on a dairy farm in Central New York. Cindy also edits for High Tide Publications and writes regular blog posts: www.cindylfreeman.blogspot.com

Website: www.cindy@cindylfreeman.com

MARY MONTAGUE SIKES is an author/artist who divides her attention between painting and writing. A former correspondent for The Newport News Daily Press and the Richmond News Leader, Sikes is the author of hundreds of published feature articles and photographs. Her paintings are in public and private collections in the United States, Canada and the Caribbean. Her book *Hearts Across Forever* (part of the "Passenger to Paradise" series) was rereleased in 2019.

Visit her website at: www.marymontaguesikes.blogspot.com

All Interests
All Levels
No Limits

About the Writers Guild of Virginia

The Writers Guild of Virginia is a 501(c)3 organization. Our mission is to nurture writers of all abilities in the craft of writing, publishing and marketing of their work. We offer a series of tuition based and free half and full-day workshops and multi-week courses throughout the Northern Neck, Middle Peninsula, and Williamsburg areas.

We hope you will visit us on our website to learn more about us and join us at one of our events.

Thank you for your support!

How to Reach Us
email:wgvirigina@gmail.com
website:www.wgviriginia.com

ISBN: 978-1-945990-33-5
First Edition 2019

Edited by Cindy L. Freeman

Published by High Tide Publications, Inc.
Deltaville, Virginia

Find us at:
www.HighTidePublications.com
Printed in the United States of America.

On The Cover:

"Behind the Hidden Door" 8" x 8"
by Mary Montague Sikes

Quote from the Artist:
I love cold wax for the mystery in the paintings!

www.ingramcontent.com/pod-product-compliance
Lightning Source LLC
Chambersburg PA
CBHW041004170626
46815CB00002B/151